PUFFIN BOOKS

PUZZLING PEOPLE

Were they real or were they not?

Have you heard of Robin Hood and Maid Marian – were they real people? And what about Florence Nightingale and Joan of Arc? And could there really have been a person called Britannia?

Well, here's a book to help you find out about lots of famous people – real and unreal. With every turn of the page you'll discover something about someone, and when you've read the whole book you'll be able to amaze your friends with your knowledge!

Scoular Anderson was born in Dunoon in Argyllshire and educated at Kiel School. He studied graphic design at Glasgow School of Art, spent a few years as artist-in-residence at London University, then taught art in secondary schools for about ten years. He is now a full-time illustrator and author.

PUZZLING PEOPLE

Scoular Anderson

PUFFIN BOOKS

PUFFIN BOOKS

Published by the Penguin Group
Penguin Books Ltd, 27 Wrights Lane, London W8 5TZ, England
Penguin Books USA Inc., 375 Hudson Street, New York, New York 10014, USA
Penguin Books Australia Ltd, Ringwood, Australia
Penguin Books Canada Ltd, 10 Alcorn Avenue, Toronto, Ontario, Canada M4V 3B2
Penguin Books (NZ) Ltd, 182–190 Wairau Road, Auckland 10, New Zealand

Penguin Books Ltd, Registered Offices: Harmondsworth, Middlesex, England

First published 1992
10 9 8 7 6 5 4 3 2 1

Filmset in Bembo

Made and printed in England by Clays Ltd, St Ives plc

CONTENTS

Tarzan

Tarzan was an English gentleman whose real name was Lord Greystoke.

When he was just a baby he was travelling with his parents on a ship which was wrecked off the African coast. The little boy was rescued and brought up by chimpanzees. Eventually he was rescued and returned to England to claim his estate.

Was he real or was he not?

No!

Tarzan was a character dreamed up by an American writer, Edgar Rice Burroughs. The first Tarzan book was written in 1913 and was the first of many Tarzan adventures. The first Tarzan film, *Tarzan of the Apes*, followed soon after. It was a silent film, first shown in 1918.

There have been over forty Tarzan films since then, and eighteen different actors have played the star part.

AL CAPONE

In the 1930s and 1940s many films were made about gangsters in the big cities of America. The films were usually full of tough guys, car chases and lots of violence. The gangsters toted Tommy Guns (short for Thompson Short-barrelled Machine Guns) which were easily hidden in violin cases!

Al Capone was often featured as the gang leader in many of those films.

> Was he real or was he not?

Yes!

Alphonse Capone was born in Brooklyn, New York, in 1899. He became a gang leader in Chicago, organizing gambling, burglary and other crimes – especially the sale of whisky. For fourteen years the sale and drinking of alcohol was banned in the USA and gangsters made a fortune from selling it illegally.

Al Capone was arrested in 1931, but people were too frightened to give evidence against him. He was finally gaoled for ten years – for not paying his tax!

Remember, Remember,
The fifth of November,
Gunpowder, treason
  and plot!

So goes the old rhyme. We remember poor old Guy Fawkes by sticking him on the top of a bonfire and setting off fireworks around him.

But was he real or was he not?

Yes!

In 1605 a group of men plotted to blow up the Houses of Parliament along with everyone inside, including the king, James I.

The cellars were filled with barrels of gunpowder. They chose 5 November to do the dirty deed and they picked poor old Guy Fawkes to light the fuse.

Unfortunately for the plotters, word of this foul plan got out. Guy Fawkes was arrested and tortured on the rack until he revealed the names of his accomplices.

Ever since then, the cellars have been searched before the opening of Parliament.

The Grand Old Duke of York...

. . . he had ten thousand men.
He marched them up to the top of the hill
And he marched them down again.

We know the Grand Old Duke of
York is a nursery rhyme character,
but . . .
Was he real or was he not?

13

The Duke wasn't old...

...he was only 30

He didn't have 10,000 men...

...no! He had 30,000!

He didn't march up a hill...

...the land was as flat as a pancake

Apart from that...

A monument 38 metres high was erected in London in his honour. Some jokers said it was to help him to get as far away from his debts as possible. He owed £2,000,000 on his death

Yes!

He was Frederick Augustus, Duke of York, the second son of George III. Although a good soldier he had one or two spots of bad luck during military campaigns – hence the rhyme.

14

Mona Lisa

The year was 1503. The place was Italy. The artist, Leonardo da Vinci, took up a fresh canvas, picked up his brushes and began to paint. He painted a beautiful woman with a mysterious smile on her face and called her Mona Lisa. Today, this is one of the most famous paintings in the world.

Was she real or was she not?

Yes!

The lady was real. She was the wife of Francesco di Bartolommeo del Gioconda, a rich merchant from Florence. Mona Lisa is short for 'Madonna Lisa' which simply means 'Lady Lisa'. The painting is sometimes called *La Gioconda*, which was the lady's surname.

It is said that Leonardo da Vinci paid singers, musicians and jesters to amuse the lady while he painted.

The unfortunate merchant Signor Gioconda had to wait four years for his wife's portrait!

A Collection of Kings ~ Good King Wenceslas Old King Cole King Arthur

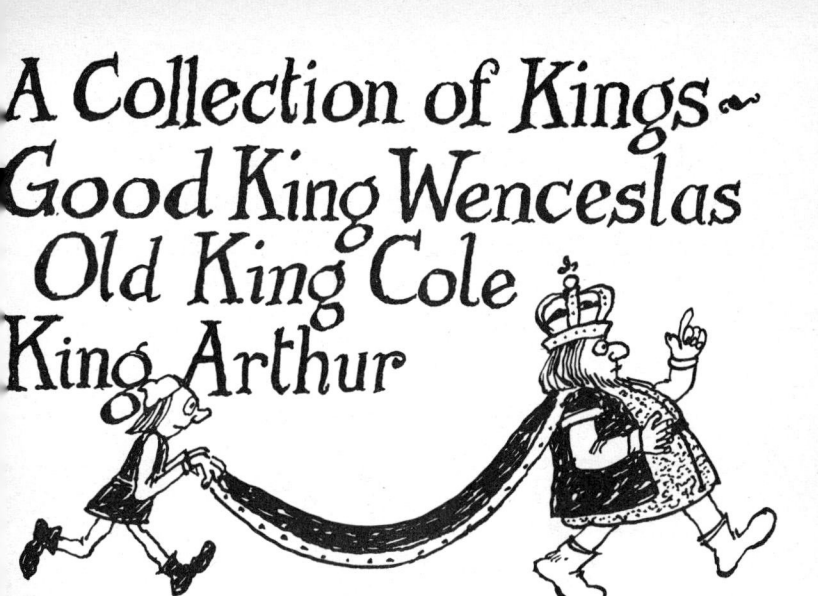

Good King Wenceslas looked out
On the feast of Stephen,
When the snow lay round about
Deep and crisp and even . . .

Old King Cole was a merry old soul
And a merry old soul was he . . .

So all day long the noise of battle roll'd
Among the mountains by the winter sea;
Until King Arthur's table, man by man,
Had fallen . . .

So were the kings in these poems real or were they not?

Wenceslas lived in the 10th century. He was duke of Bohemia (Czechoslovakia today), and a very religious man. Poor Wenceslas was murdered by his brother Boleslav. The main square in Prague, the capital of Czechoslovakia, is called Wenceslas Square.

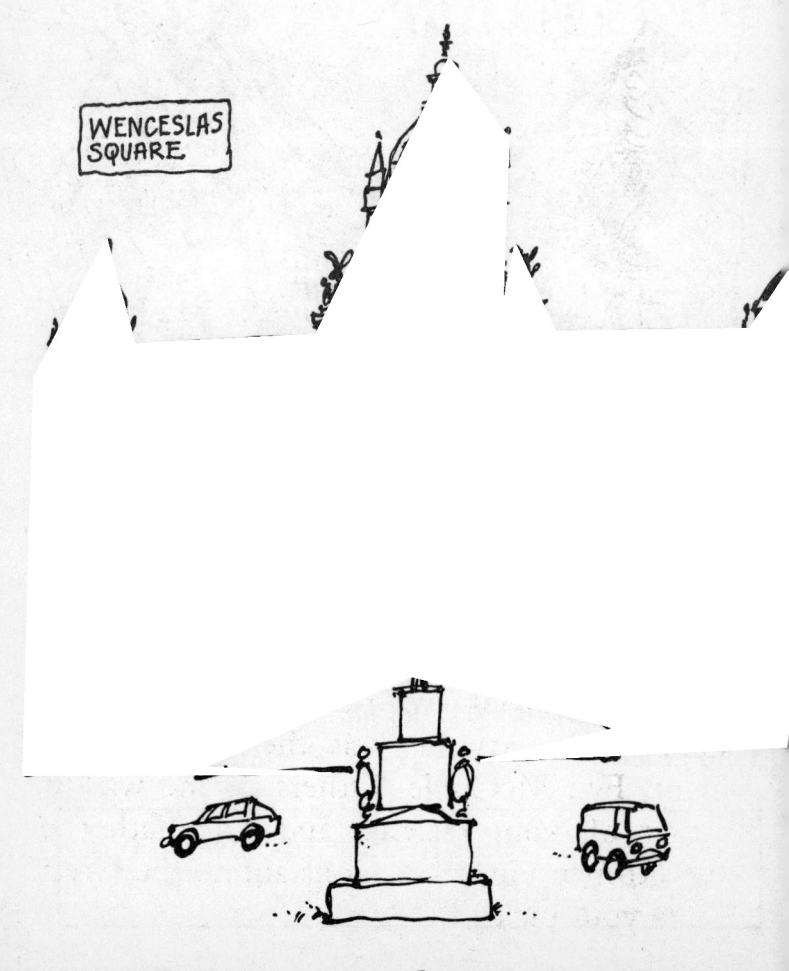

We know that King Cole called for his pipe and called for his bowl (of wine), and he liked music because he had fiddlers three!

But people can't seem to agree who he really was. Some say he was the king that built the town of Colchester. Others say he wasn't a king at all but a tailor from Reading called Colebrook, whose nickname was Old Cole. Some say he was the father of the giant, Fyn McCoule. Others say he was the father of Saint Helena, and grandfather of the Roman emperor, Constantine the Great. Take your pick!

King Arthur is a very shadowy figure. Some people say he is only a legend, while others say he definitely lived.

His name first appears around AD 500 and he is described as a brave king who won many battles. Whether he was real or not, there are many exciting stories about King Arthur; his beautiful Queen, Guinevere; the noble knight, Sir Lancelot; the magic sword, Excalibur and the wizard Merlin. (Merlin is usually thought of as a very old man but some say he was a young boy with magical powers.)

According to legend, King Arthur is lying under the ground, in a place called Avalon, ready to rise with his band of warriors when his country needs him.

Walt Disney

Walt Disney cartoons are often seen on television and in the cinema. They were the first films to use moving cartoons instead of real actors.

In 1928 Walt Disney had a great success with a character called Mortimer Mouse in the film *Steamboat Willie*.

MOUSE AUDITIONS

None of them are any good

But was Walt Disney real or was he not?

Yes!

Walt Disney invented Mortimer Mouse – who later became Mickey Mouse – and many other characters: Donald Duck, Goofy and Pluto, to name a few.

In 1937 he brought out his first full-length cartoon film, *Snow White and the Seven Dwarfs*. The film needed over 100,000 separate drawings during its making!

THE HUNCHBACK OF NOTRE-DAME

The Hunchback of Notre-Dame was a deformed creature who lived in one of the towers of Notre-Dame Cathedral in Paris. He once swung down from his tower on a rope and rescued a young woman who was about to be burned at the stake.

Was he real or was he not?

No!

Quasimodo was his name and he appeared in a novel called *Notre-Dame de Paris* by the French writer, Victor Hugo. Quasimodo was the bell-ringer of Notre-Dame cathedral and he fell in love with a beautiful gypsy girl called Esmerelda.

Two of Victor Hugo's other novels have been set to music. *Le Roi S'amuse* was retitled *Rigoletto* and became a famous opera by the Italian composer, Giuseppe Verdi and *Les Miserables* became a musical in the 1980s.

Robin Hood

Robin Hood was Robert Fitzooth, the outlawed Earl of Huntingdon, (otherwise known as Robin of Loxley). He lived in Sherwood Forest with his band of men and robbed the rich to feed the poor.

Right, my fat friend, hand over your purse!

Was he real or was he not?

No!

Robin Hood is said to have lived during the reign of King Richard I – he's also said to have lived during the reign of Edward II. That would make him about 140 years old! Some stories say that Robin Hood lived in Yorkshire while others say he lived in Nottinghamshire.

But the truth is that he never lived at all!

The tales of Robin Hood and his band of merry men are still as popular today as they were 800 years ago. Robin's companions were Little John, Will Scarlet, Much, Allen-a-Dale, George-a-Green, Friar Tuck and Maid Marian.

In past centuries, May Day was sometimes known as Robin Hood's Day. People skipped round the maypole and the dancers in the Morris Dance represented Robin and his merry men.

Cinderella

Once there was a rich man who had a lovely wife and a beautiful daughter called Cinderella. Sadly, his first wife died and he married again – a mean and bad-tempered woman who had two rather stuck-up daughters. They made life very difficult for Cinderella. They expected her to cook and clean, while they dressed up in fine clothes . . .

Is the story of Cinderella based on a real person?

No!

It's just a fairy-tale.

The story of Cinderella (and sometimes known as Cinder Slut) is as old as the hills and versions of it can be found in many countries. It became a favourite tale when it appeared in a collection of French fairy-tales called *Mother Goose Stories* in 1697.

By the way, have you ever wondered how uncomfortable (or downright dangerous!) Cinderella's glass slippers must have been? Well, it has been said that there was a mix-up between the French words *verre* (meaning glass) and *vair* (meaning fur) when the story was translated.

JULIUS CAESAR

Julius Caesar was a famous Roman statesman, general and historian. He was stabbed to death by his enemies on the Ides of March (15 March). William Shakespeare wrote a play about him.

Was he real or was he not?

Yes!

When he was twenty-three, Gaius Julius Caesar was kidnapped by pirates and held to ransom. As soon as the money was paid and he was set free, he gathered an army, killed the pirates and used the ransom money to pay his soldiers. That shows you what sort of man he was!

He was described as tall, thin-featured, bald and clean-shaven. With his skill as a politician and an army general he rapidly gained promotion. In 48 BC he was made 'dictator' of the Roman empire, though he really wanted to be king.

His enemies decided he was getting too big for his boots and stabbed him to death on the steps of the parliament building.

I've just washed them, mate!

The PIED PIPER of HAMELIN

The year was 1284. The place was the town of Hamelin in Germany. The townsfolk didn't know what to do because the town was overrun with rats. A man appeared and offered to get rid of the rats and, in return, the townsfolk promised to pay him well. The man walked out of town and the rats followed – but the townsfolk refused to pay him.

The next day he played his pipe again and this time all the children followed him out of the town – never to be seen again.

> Was he real or was he not?

No!

The Pied Piper of Hamelin is just a legend but the story might have been inspired by the Children's Crusade which took place in 1212. A man called Nicholas of Cologne persuaded 40,000 children to go with him on a pilgrimage to the Holy Land. The whole thing ended in disaster. Those that managed the long journey to Italy (where they were to get a boat to the Holy Land) were ordered home by Pope Pius III.

SHERLOCK HOLMES

Sherlock Holmes was a famous detective who lived at 221B Baker Street, London. He solved many difficult crimes at the end of the last century. He was known as a very observant man – he believed that every hair and speck of dust could be a vital clue.

Good grief, it's a piece of toast! I deduce it must be breakfast time!

Was he real or was he not?

No!

Many people wrote to Sherlock Holmes at 221B Baker Street because he seemed so real – but he wasn't!

This famous detective was invented by Sir Arthur Conan Doyle, a writer born in Edinburgh in 1859. He studied medicine and modelled Sherlock Holmes on several of his medical professors.

The Hound of the Baskervilles is just one of the many Sherlock Holmes books and 'Elementary, my dear Watson,' became his catch-phrase. (Dr Watson was a friend who helped him solve his cases.)

Sir Arthur Conan Doyle eventually grew tired of his creation and tried to kill off Holmes by making him fall over a cliff. The outcry from readers was so great that he had to bring Holmes back to life again!

HANNIBAL

Hannibal was a general who marched his army – plus thirty-seven elephants – over the Alps from France to Italy.

Is this true or is it not?

Yes!

Hannibal – which means 'the grace of god Baal' – was a general from Carthage. Carthage stood on the north coast of Africa, directly opposite the city of Rome in Italy. Hannibal's father made him swear that the Roman Empire would be his enemy for ever.

Hannibal set out to fight the Romans. Firstly he fought them in Spain, then he headed for Italy across the treacherous Alps. His men (and his elephants) were used to a hot climate so many of them died in the ice and snow of the mountain passes. Although Hannibal was a great general he failed to defeat Rome.

He eventually poisoned himself to escape capture.

CLEOPATRA

Cleopatra was queen of Egypt and one of the most beautiful women in the world. She died when she was bitten by a snake smuggled to her in a basket of figs. (She was in prison at the time.)

Was she real or was she not?

Yes!

Cleopatra was real and lived from about 50 BC to 30 BC. Her enemies said she used her beauty to catch important men and use their power. She certainly had a love affair with Julius Caesar and with another Roman general, Mark Antony.

The Romans wanted to get rid of Cleopatra – they defeated Antony and Cleopatra's army at the battle of Actium. Antony was made to believe that Cleopatra had killed herself so he tried to commit suicide by falling on his sword. He died later in Cleopatra's arms.

Then Cleopatra killed herself – some say she was bitten by an asp (a small snake), others say she was bitten by a cobra (a large snake), and yet others say by taking poison she kept hidden in a hollow comb.

DRACULA

Count Dracula lived in Transylvania, which is part of Romania. He was known for his nasty habit of riding round the country at night and biting people in the neck!

But did he exist or not?

No!

Dracula was the vampire in a novel written by Bram Stoker and published in 1897. Bram Stoker may have got his bloodthirsty idea from the story of the king of Wallachia (also in Romania) nicknamed Vlad the Impaler.

The kings of Wallachia had a dragon fighting a unicorn on their coat-of-arms. They also took the name Dracul – meaning dragon. After a battle with the Turks, Vlad impaled 3,000 captives on stakes by the river.

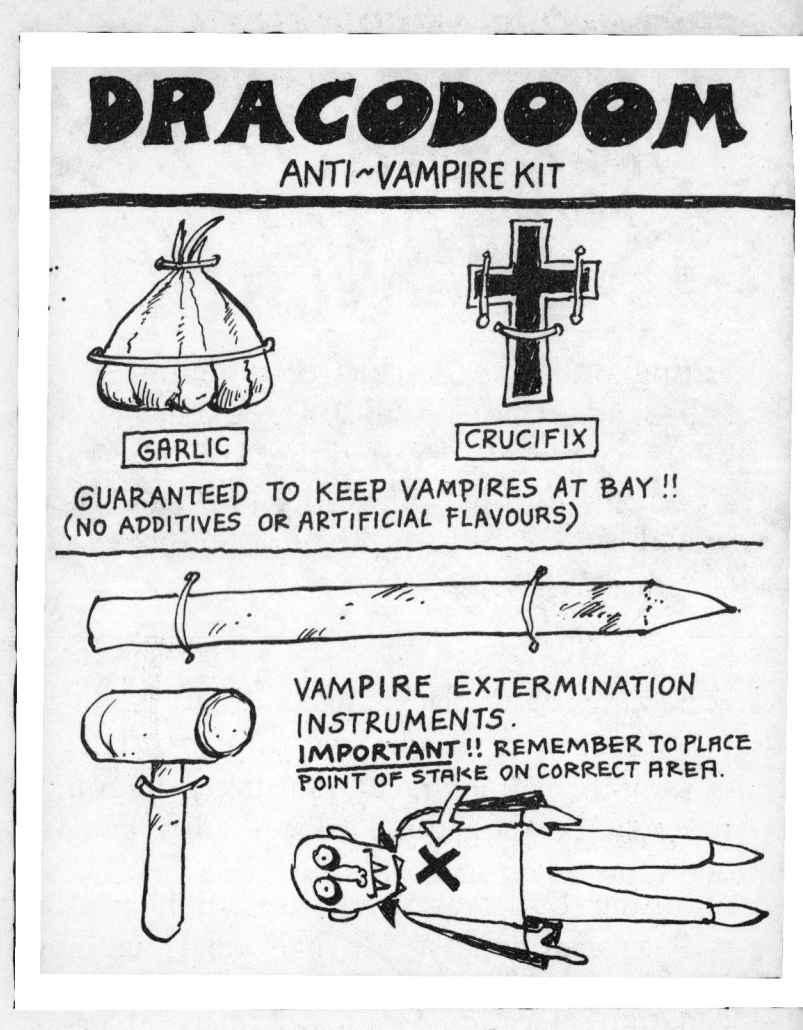

The first Dracula film was made in 1931. It starred the actor Bela Lugosi who often gave interviews while lying in a coffin. He asked that his Dracula cape be buried with him when he died.

TWO NATIVE AMERICANS
CHIEF SITTING BULL AND HIAWATHA

Sitting Bull was the chief of the Hunk Papa tribe and eventually became leader of the Sioux nation. He defeated the American cavalry at the Battle of Little Big Horn and then joined Buffalo Bill's Wild West Show.

Sitting Bull was a warrior but Hiawatha was a peace-maker. He had many strange adventures but went among the Indian tribes bringing goodwill and persuading them to live in peace with each other.

Were they real or were they not?

Yes!

Sitting Bull certainly did fight the American cavalry. The battle was also known as Custer's Last Stand because General George Custer and all his 270 men were slaughtered by the Indians.

Sitting Bull was pretty cruel to other Indian tribes, too. Once he killed everyone in a village but spared one boy because of his bravery and adopted him as his brother. Later, he joined Buffalo Bill and his travelling circus.

No!

Hiawatha is a myth. He was the miraculous hero of the Iroquois tribe. His mother was the squaw Winonah and his father was the Mudjikeewis, the west wind. The legend was made famous in a poem by Henry Longfellow called *The Song of Hiawatha*.

JEKYLL & HYDE

These two men were in fact one!

Dr Henry Jekyll was a clever scientist who invented a special potion which could completely change his looks and personality. He called his other 'self' Mr Edward Hyde.

Was he real or was he not?

No!

The Strange Case of Dr Jekyll and Mr Hyde was written by Robert Louis Stevenson (who also wrote *Treasure Island*) in 1886.

The story has been a favourite one for film-makers. In films, Mr Hyde is usually shown as a raging, hairy monster. In the book he is simply described as being young, stocky and of a strange countenance.

WILD WEST HEROES
BUFFALO BILL
DAVY CROCKET
THE LONE RANGER

Buffalo Bill first worked for the Pony Express but he earned his name from hunting buffalo. He's said to have killed over 4,000 animals, single-handed in a year and a half.

Davy Crocket was a well-known marksman, fighter and bear-hunter. He was also a lawyer and was elected to the American Congress (parliament).

The Lone Ranger was a cowboy who wandered the wild west fighting crime and bringing criminals to justice. He wore a mask to hide a scar on his face.

Were they real or were they not?

BUFFALO BILL'S WILD WEST SHOW

THRILLING SHARP-SHOOTING

EXCITING LARIAT-WHIRLING

Yes!

Buffalo Bill's real name was William Frederick Cody. He hunted buffalo to provide meat for the gangs of labourers constructing the Kansas Pacific Railroad.

He toured America and Europe with his Wild West Show which told the story of the settlers in America. There were also spectacular displays from Indians, cowboys and cowgirls, bucking broncos and trick riders.

Yes!

David Crocket was real, too. He was elected to represent the state of Tennessee in 1821. He always wore a racoon-skin hat and called his favourite rifle 'Betsy'.

He was killed while helping to defend the Alamo, a fort in Texas. It was besieged for thirteen days in 1836 by the Mexicans who eventually wiped out the entire garrison.

No!

The Lone Ranger wasn't a real person. He was the hero of a popular TV series. His horse was called Silver and he had an Indian companion called Tonto. The Lone Ranger had been injured on the face by a bullet and was determined to bring to justice the man who had shot him.

JOAN of ARC

When Joan of Arc was thirteen she started hearing voices. She persuaded the French king that she had been sent to help the French in their hour of need. Then she dressed as a man and led the French to victory over the English army.

Was she real or was she not?

Yes!

Joan was born in 1412. Her parents were poor peasants. She said the voices she heard belonged to Saint Margaret, Saint Catherine and Saint Michael and they told her to drive the English from French soil.

She inspired the French soldiers to victory but a year later she was captured by the English. She was interrogated, tortured and accused of being a witch. The English eventually burnt her at the stake. She was made a Roman Catholic saint in 1920.

ROBINSON CRUSOE

Robinson Crusoe was a sailor who was shipwrecked on a remote island. He was a very practical man and managed to look after himself for twenty-eight years, two months and nineteen days before being rescued. He made friends with a native he called Friday.

Was he real or was he not?

No!

Robinson Crusoe was, in fact, a character in a book by Daniel Defoe. The book was published in 1719 and its full title was *The Life and Strange Surprising Adventures of Robinson Crusoe, of York, Mariner, Written by Himself.*

However, the book *was* based on the real story of a Scottish sailor, Alexander Selkirk. During a voyage he quarrelled with the captain, the pirate William Dampier. Selkirk asked to be put ashore and was abandoned on the island of Juan Fernandez in the Pacific Ocean. He survived for five years (not the twenty-eight in the book!) before being rescued.

TWO STRONG MEN

HERCULES and CHARLES ATLAS

Both Hercules and Charles Atlas were men of incredible strength. They were famed for their huge muscles and powerful feats.

Were they real or were they not?

No!

Hercules and the tales of his strength exist only in Greek legend. In a fit of madness he killed his family, so Zeus (the chief god) punished him by setting him twelve almost impossible tasks. Most of which involved catching wild animals or monsters.

Yes!

Charles Atlas, on the other hand, was real. He perfected a method of building up his muscles and was the first body-builder to become famous. He used to advertise his method of body-building by showing a skinny man on the beach, having sand kicked in his face – but if the man had had a body like Charles Atlas, of course, this would never happen!

He took the name 'Atlas' from another of the giants in Greek legend. Atlas was also punished by Zeus – he had to hold the heavens on his shoulders for eternity.

By the way, a book of maps is called an Atlas because one of the first books, published in 1595, had a picture of Atlas on the front page.

A Trio of Pirates
CAPTAIN KIDD
CAPTAIN HOOK
LONG JOHN SILVER

Many expeditions have visited the islands of the West Indies in search of 'Kidd's Treasure'. Captain Kidd was a very successful pirate who was supposed to have buried most of his treasure. He was hanged for knocking a sailor on the head with a bucket.

Captain Hook was described as being very much a gentleman, with long black curly hair and blue eyes. In place of a right hand he had a hook which he used to kill members of his crew who annoyed him.

Long John Silver was a cook. He was very tall and strong, with a broad, pale face. His left leg was cut off close to the hip and under his left shoulder he carried a crutch. He used the crutch to hop quickly about like a bird.

Did they live or did they not?

Yes!

Captain William Kidd lived from 1645 to 1701. The British government tried to change him from a pirate into a catcher of pirates by bribing him with the offer of a ship. But old habits die hard and when he entered the port of Boston in America, after yet another piratical voyage, he was arrested. He wasn't charged with piracy, though. He was condemned to death for killing a mutinous sailor by hitting him on the head with a bucket.

No!

Captain Hook was a pirate only in the book *Peter Pan*! Although he was a fearless and terrifying pirate, he became a lump of jelly when he heard the sound of the tick-tocking crocodile. He met his end in the crocodile's huge jaws.

No!

Long John Silver was the well-known seaman in Robert Louis Stevenson's book *Treasure Island*. At the beginning of the story he was an innkeeper in Bristol, having lost his leg in a sea-battle. Then, in search of treasure, with the young Jim Hawkins, he went to sea as a cook aboard the *Hispaniola*. But before long he returned to his piratical ways . . .

King Canute

The English king, Canute, once had his throne carried down to the sea-shore. He sat down and tried to order the tide to turn.

Was he real or was he not?

Yes!

Canute, or Cnut, was King of England from 1016 to 1035. He was also King of Denmark and Norway.

To begin with he was rather a ruthless ruler, known for chopping off the noses, ears and hands of his captives. He finally settled down to be a good king and brought peace to his lands.

When some of his courtiers began to flatter him too much he went down to the beach and showed that the tide didn't take orders even from a great king.

Romeo and Juliet

In the Italian City of Verona there were two wealthy families, the Capulets and the Montagues. The families hated each other and there were often brawls in the streets between their servants.

But unfortunately, young Juliet Capulet loved Romeo Montague. They were married in secret – which led to a tragic end . . .

Were these famous lovers real or were they not?

No!

The characters of one of the most famous love stories were not real. They appear in Shakespeare's play *Romeo and Juliet*. At the end of the story Romeo poisons himself and Juliet stabs herself. When the two families see what their hatred has caused, they make peace with each other.

The musical *West Side Story* by Leonard Bernstein is a modern version of the same story set in New York.

BRITANNIA

The lady called Britannia appears on our fifty pence piece wearing a helmet, holding a trident and with a lion and shield by her side. She has appeared on coins for centuries.

But who was this lady? Was she real or was she not?

No!

Rule Britannia, Britannia rules the waves,
Britons never, never, never shall be slaves!

So goes the old song – but Britannia was not a real person.

The countries of England, Scotland and Wales were called Britannia by Julius Caesar. The picture of a woman with a shield representing Britannia first appeared on Roman coins in AD 161.

She reappeared on coins during the reign of Charles II. In this case a real person – the Duchess of Richmond – sat as a model for the coin engraver, Mr Roetier.

DICK TURPIN

It was a black night on Hounslow Heath. A dark, masked figure appeared sitting on a black horse. He drew out a pistol and stopped a passing coach.

'Your money or your life!' he demanded.

Was it the famous highwayman Dick Turpin? Or was it only the local butcher having a lark?

Was Dick Turpin real or was he not?

Yes!

Dick Turpin was real – and he was a butcher!

In 1728 he set himself up as a butcher in Essex. He began to steal sheep and cattle to stock his shop. Then he tried his hand at housebreaking and smuggling on the River Thames.

By the age of thirty he had become a highwayman in the countryside around London. His daring raids made him a legend and he became known as the 'King of the Road'.

In 1737 the call went out for his arrest.

WANTED
RICHARD TURPIN

HE IS ABOUT THIRTY-FIVE, FIVE FEET
NINE INCHES HIGH, BROWN COMPLEXION,
VERY MUCH MARKED WITH SMALL-POX,
HIS CHEEK-BONES BROAD, HIS FACE
THINNER TOWARDS THE BOTTOM,
HIS VISAGE SHORT AND PRETTY
UPRIGHT AND BROAD ABOUT THE
SHOULDERS.

Dick Turpin made a spectacular ride on his horse, Black Bess, from London to York. He had been accused of yet another crime in London. He wanted to prove he had been in York at the time, though it's doubtful that he could have ridden all the way to York on one horse, without stopping, in such a quick time.

The law caught up with him in the end and he was hanged in York at the age of thirty-four.

JAMES BOND

James Bond was a secret agent. He travelled to every corner of the world working as a spy for the British Government. He narrowly escaped death more than once during his undercover operations and many films have been made about his daring missions.

Was he real or was he not?

No!

Many films have been made about James Bond but he wasn't real.

He was a character created by the writer Ian Fleming. The first James Bond adventure *Casino Royale* was published in 1952. It was followed by twelve others. The first James Bond film was *Dr No* which came out in 1962.

Madame Tussaud

It was the time of the French Revolution.

In Paris the blade of the guillotine fell with a horrible slithering sound. Another unfortunate person had lost his head. Beside the scaffold a young woman was taking wax impressions of the faces of the dead.

Some years later she opened a waxworks to show off some of these faces.

"This isn't going to hurt, is it?"

WAXING KIT

Was she real or was she not?

Yes!

Marie Tussaud was born in France. Her mother was housekeeper to Dr Curtius who had a wax museum in Paris. He taught Marie to model likenesses in wax and left his museum to her when he died.

During the Revolution, the authorities made her take impressions of the faces of the important people who had been guillotined – like Queen Marie Antoinette, for instance.

Marie Tussaud moved to England and toured Britain with her wax exhibition of heroes and rogues. She set up a permanent display in London near where Madame Tussaud's stands today.

Casanova

When a man flirts with a woman you might sometimes hear people call him 'a right little Casanova!'

Casanova lived during the eighteenth century. He was a playboy who travelled the length and breadth of Europe, always with a beautiful woman on his arm.

But was he real or was he not?

Yes!

Giovanni Jacopo Casanova de Seingalt, knight of the Golden Spur, was born in Venice.

He must have taken an interest in the ladies early in his life because he was expelled from school for immoral behaviour. He spent his life wandering round the capital cities of Europe, mixing with aristocrats and wealthy people. He was imprisoned in Venice for a while but he escaped.

He earned money by being a diplomat, a priest, a gambler, a cardinal's secretary, a violinist and a spy. He eventually ended up as librarian to Count Waldstein in Bohemia (Czechoslovakia today) where he died at the ripe old age of seventy-three.

Mary Poppins

The film *Mary Poppins* was based on the life story of a woman who became a nanny to a large family at the beginning of this century. She was a thin woman with dark hair who always carried a big bag and an umbrella, and turned out to be a nanny with strange powers.

Was she real or was she not?

No!

The character was invented by the writer P. L. Travers who was born in Australia in 1906. She moved to England when she was seventeen. She worked as an actress and a dancer before she took up writing. She wrote *Mary Poppins* when she was twenty-eight. The Walt Disney film was made in 1964.

SINBAD
THE SAILOR

Sinbad was a wealthy citizen of Baghdad who went to sea on seven voyages. He found many riches during his travels but he also had some hair-raising adventures – he was shipwrecked several times!

Not again!

Was he real or was he not?

No!

There was once a king called Shahriyar who killed each of his wives the day after their marriage. He got through a lot of wives! At last, one wife, called Sheherezade, managed to put off her execution by telling the king a story – and another, and another – every night for one thousand and one nights.

The story of Sinbad the Sailor was just one of the tales she told, so Sinbad was not real. But neither was Sheherezade! All this is just one big fairy story. *The Tales of a Thousand and One Nights* were written down in Arabic over a thousand years ago – which must make them among the oldest stories in the world.

A giant whale, a huge bird that could lift an elephant and an island of hairy dwarfs were just a few of the things Sinbad came across on his adventures.

Boudicca
or Boadicea

Boudicca was an English warrior queen who fixed swords to her chariot wheels. This made a bit of a mess when the Roman soldiers didn't get their feet out of the way quickly.

Was she real or was she not?

Yes!

Boudicca lived in the first century AD. She was queen of the Iceni tribe in Eastern England. When the Romans invaded her lands they ill-treated her so she gathered an army and marched on London. Her army is said to have killed over 70,000 Romans. In the end she was defeated and took her own life with poison.

A DESCRIPTION OF BOUDICCA BY A ROMAN HISTORIAN:

SHE WAS VERY TALL, IN APPEARANCE, TERRIFYING, IN THE GLANCE OF HER EYE MOST FIERCE, AND HER VOICE WAS HARSH.
A GREAT MASS OF THE TAWNIEST HAIR FELL TO HER HIPS. AROUND HER NECK SHE WORE A LARGE GOLDEN NECKLACE AND SHE WORE A TUNIC OF DIVERSE COLOURS OVER WHICH A THICK MANTLE WAS FASTENED WITH A BROOCH.

The Scarlet Pimpernel

We seek him here, we seek him there,
Those Frenchies seek him everywhere.
Is he in heaven? – or is he in hell?
That damned elusive pimpernel?

The Scarlet Pimpernel was really Sir Percy Blakeney. He was a secret agent who rescued hundreds of people from the guillotine during the French Revolution and smuggled them across the channel to England.

Sacre bleu! She was here a second ago!

WHOOOSH!

Was he real or was he not?

No!

Sir Percy Blakeney was known as the Scarlet Pimpernel because he chose a little wild flower, the scarlet Pimpernel, as his emblem.

But he was only the hero of a book. It was written in 1902 by Baroness Orczy, (Emma Magdalena Rosalia Marie Sofia Barbara to her friends). She was a Hungarian who settled in England.

LADY GODIVA

A lady well-known for her stunt of riding naked through the town of Coventry on her horse.

Did she do it or did she not?

Yes!

In 1040, her husband, Leofric, Earl of Mercia and Lord of Coventry, rather unkindly raised the taxes of the people of Coventry. When his wife objected to this, Leofric said, that if she rode naked from one end of the town to the other, he would lower the taxes again. He didn't think she would do it – but she did! The townsfolk showed their appreciation by hiding in their houses so she wouldn't be seen.

Another ending was added to the story much later. A tailor called Tom couldn't resist peeking through his keyhole as Lady Godiva passed by. He was struck blind in one eye and was known ever after as 'Peeping Tom'.

THREE MONSTROUS TERRORS
GENGHIS KHAN ATTILA THE HUN KING KONG

The warrior Genghis Khan was leader of the Mongols. When he conquered new lands he left pyramids of skulls to warn people what would happen if they fought back.

Attila the Hun was every bit as terrible – if not worse – than Genghis Khan. Fortunately, he met his early end when he choked on a chicken bone during his wedding feast.

The most terrifying of all – King Kong – was a giant ape which got loose in New York in 1933 and created havoc.

Were they real or were they not?

Yes!

Genghis Khan was real. He succeeded his father as king of the Mongols at the age of thirteen. He changed his name from Temujin to Genghis Khan which means 'Very Mighty Ruler'.

EVEN TODAY, MONGOL WRESTLERS HAVE BANNERS WITH GENGHIS KHAN'S PORTRAIT ON THEM AS THEY STILL REGARD HIM AS THEIR GREAT LEADER.

The Chinese had built the Great Wall of China to keep the Mongols out but Genghis and his armies flooded over it easily. He managed to conquer most of Asia and it was said that it took two years to cross his empire on horseback.

When he died, his soldiers killed anyone who saw the funeral procession because they wanted his death kept secret.

Yes!

Attila lived about 700 years before Genghis. He was King of the Huns, a tribe that lived in Eastern Europe. They conquered many lands, from China in the east, to parts of France and Italy in the west.

He had just married Ildeco, a princess from Burgundy, when he took that fateful large mouthful . . .

No!

King Kong wasn't a king and he wasn't real! He was the giant hairy ape that struck terror into New Yorkers in the film *King Kong* which came out in 1933.

In 1956 the Japanese brought out a film about another monster, the creature 'Godzilla'. In 1963 the two monsters starred in the film *King Kong Versus Godzilla*. In the Japanese version of the film, Godzilla wins – but in the American version, King Kong wins. Naturally!

SAINT GEORGE
...and the dragon

Saint George was a brave knight who is said to have defeated, single-handed, a monster, possibly a dragon. He is the patron saint of England (and of Portugal, boy scouts and soldiers).

Was he real or was he not?

Yes!

He was real but there are some arguments about his true identity. Some say he was George, Bishop of Alexandria in Egypt. Others say he was a Roman soldier. As for the dragon – it never existed. The dragon is just a symbol of evil. Whenever a picture shows Saint George fighting a dragon – he is really trying to wipe out evil. (Other saints were shown as dragon-slayers, too: St Michael, St Margaret, St Samson, St Clement, St Romain, St Philip, St Martha, St Florent, St Cado, St Maudet, St Pol and St Keyne all had a go!)

Florence Nightingale

She was a nurse and was known as the 'Lady with the Lamp' because she used to go round her hospital each night and make sure her patients were comfortable.

Is this true or is it not?

Yes!

At the age of thirty-four she went, with thirty-eight nurses, to tend the 10,000 wounded during the Crimean War (this was in Russia in 1854).

She was aware that bad hygiene was the cause of much disease and death and tried to improve hospital conditions. On her return to England she was given £50,000 to set up a nursing school.

Here are some notes she made in her diary about her nurses:

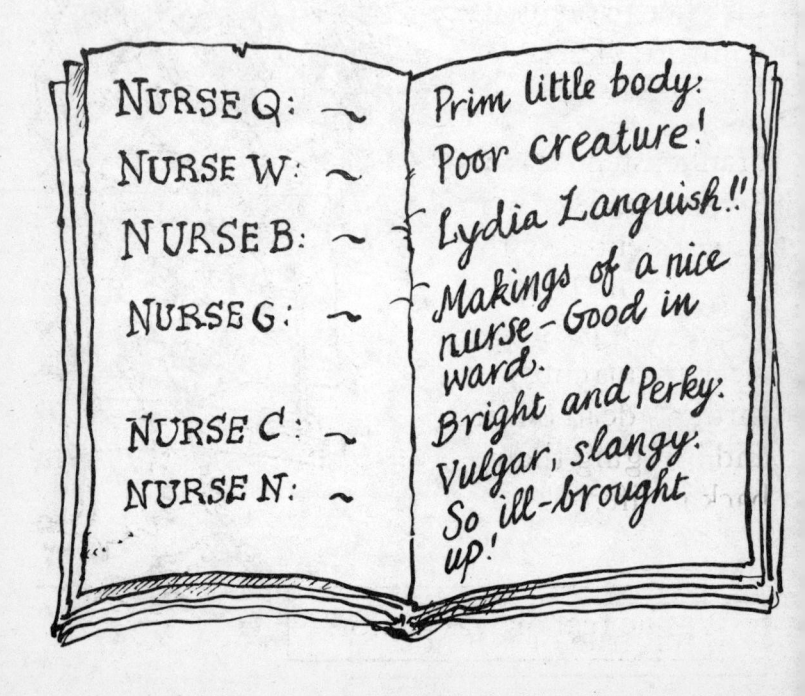

NURSE Q: ~ Prim little body.

NURSE W: ~ Poor creature!

NURSE B: ~ { Lydia Languish!"

NURSE G: ~ { Makings of a nice nurse — Good in ward.

NURSE C: ~ Bright and Perky.

NURSE N: ~ Vulgar, slangy. So ill-brought up!

FRANKENSTEIN

Frankenstein was a Swiss professor who experimented with Galvanism. That's a method of passing electric currents through dead bodies and bringing them back to life.

Was he real or was he not?

No!

It's only a story and was written by Mary Shelley and first published in 1818. She wrote it as an entry for a ghost story competition. It tells the tale of a young student who created a creature using bits of corpses from graveyards. He brought it to life by passing a bolt of lightning through it. The creature wanted friends but naturally, everyone was terrified by it.

Frankenstein realized he must kill his creation. He chased it round the world but the monster walked off into the snow of the Arctic and was never seen again.